Unwrap Your
DREAMS

Decode the Gifts of the Intuitive Realm
and Navigate Your Life with Clarity,
Joy and Compassion

Kirsten Bridge

Copyright © 2023 by Kirsten Bridge

All rights reserved. No part of this publication may be reproduced, distributed or transmitted in any form or by any means, including photocopying, recording, or other electronic or mechanical methods, without the prior written permission of the publisher, except in the case of brief quotations embodied in critical reviews and certain other noncommercial uses permitted by copyright law. For permission requests, write to the author, at: info@kirstenbridge.com

You can also find Kirsten on Instagram @kirstenlbridge

Editor: Madison Hamill

Typesetting: Glenn Bontrager (www.fiverr.com/sarco2000)

Cover Image Photographer: Raghav Modi on Unsplash

Book cover designer: Sofia da Silva

Self Published by Tiny Bear Book Press

Unwrap Your Dreams/ Kirsten Bridge
1st ed.

ISBN: 978-0-473-55358-6

Dedication

I dedicate this book to the inner mystic in you, the one who is ready to fly free into the Twilight Threshold and bring back the messages you need most right now.

Acknowledgements

I believe tiny books can make a big impact on the world because they are quick to offer insights or tools we need most.

What I didn't believe was that it would take 2 years to write something so small! I am humbled by my slow and messy process. Interestingly, I think I am wiser for taking the slow train to write this book. The additional time allowed me to know the nuances of using these processes for guidance.

Mom, thank you for being my editor of the initial, raw draft. You were the first place that I could safely land my book dream. I trusted you would tell me the truth and you did. I know that you selflessly gave time to this book. Thank you.

Alexandra Franzen, your practical approach to creativity inspired me to write a tiny book. Your teaching style asked me to trust my unique way with writing. Thank you.

Dallas Travers, I am amazed by your ability to simplify what feels complicated to communicate. Thank you for helping me to see the stance I take with my coaching. I had way more fun polishing this book with a clearer message. Thank you.

I want to thank the teachers on my spiritual journey that helped me to evolve into the woman I am today. Sherry Kramer, Martha Beck, Catriona MacGregor, John Broomfield and especially Denise Linn.

There are a few friends that have supported me on my journey by continually holding up a mirror and telling me (practically yelling) to stand taller in my role as a spiritual mentor because you saw things that I took for granted. Some of you have been encouraging me since I was a teenager. Thank you, Seeley, Kate A, Robyn, Kate F, Tina, and Dziwe and more.

To my editor, Madison Hamill. I never thought the editing process could be so energizing. Thank you.

Catriona Ferguson, I trusted you to be my first friend to read my book. I value your brilliant mind and your support. I love you for saying, "let's have a book launch party!" There is no way I would want to do this book journey without you.

Roger, my husband, we joke that you don't understand why people buy spiritual or self-help books. Yet, you stand by my side quietly supporting me. You have my back when I feel lost in my work. Thank you for saying you are excited to read this book. I appreciate that you hold space for me to do me.

Celia and Katelyn, being your mother has inspired me to be the fullest version of who I am. I have dug deep to live my dreams and still keep it real. I hope that writing this book shows you that at different stages of life you will do new things.

To the people I did the dreamwork with to prepare this book, you know who you are. Your names were changed for this book to protect your privacy. Thank you for sharing your dreams and your vulnerability with me. Not all of you are in the book's examples but you are in between the words of these pages supporting the message of this book. Thank you.

Finally, to the women that have let me mentor and teach you in The Radiant Women, I thank you. Without you I would not have the confidence to go forward into the world to share my writing or expand my work. I will see you by the fire— arriving on the 9.5 train dressed in your most ceremonial garments to celebrate this book.

Infinite love and gratitude.

Contents

Acknowledgements..................................v

Introduction.................................... 1

Using this book 5

1. Let us have a little conversation with your dream..... 9

2. Get in the driver's seat with your nightmare........ 23

3. The tiniest fragment of a dream can speak volumes .. 33

4. Become the movie director of your life and dreams .. 39

5. Take it further and enter the Twilight Threshold on your own.. 47

Conclusion..................................... 51

Introduction

When you solely place value on rational thinking, you may assume that paying attention to dream states is pointless; that they are inherently illogical and of no help in real-life problem-solving. However, relying solely on the material, objective world means you can miss the gifts of the intuitive realm of dreams that are essential to your growth.

I believe that working with dreams, leaning into your intuition and interpreting messages from the in-between states of mind are underutilized tools in society. By learning the skills to re-enter a dream you had, or enter a liminal state of mind, you access seeds of knowledge and strength that sit just outside the logical world. This book teaches you how to resource the inner world of dreams and intuition, so you can navigate your life with more clarity, joy and compassion. There is a version of trusting your inner mystic *and* using rational knowledge that is doable, sustainable and nourishing for you.

The women and techniques in the following chapters will empower you to find a balance between mystical and practical responses to difficult times in life. You will read about Sofia, who goes from a fear of flying to feeling joy when the plane takes off because she valued one of her dreams and examined it further. You'll learn how Celia discovers she is at the edge of an emotional and spiritual awakening when she courageously faces a nightmare. Finally, you will see how to use the Twilight

Threshold[1] from a waking state so that you can transform a frustrating situation into a more harmonious situation, as Shyla does for herself and her friend.

As a little girl, I used to lie in bed and drift away to complex worlds that I had created in my mind. In fact, my aunt and my mom often wondered what I was doing when I was lying so quietly on my bed for hours. I was not sleeping but I was not in an active, alert state either. In those childhood years, I learned the power of the imaginal realm and how viscerally connected we are to the possibilities we dream of. What I saw and felt in the liminal space of imagination became easier to replicate and implement. For instance, when I did not like the way a conversation happened, I simply imagined doing it over again until I liked how the dialogue felt. What may have looked like foolish daydreaming in childhood was the early stage of developing skills to work with the imaginal realm that would support me in my waking life. When I look back, knowing I could re-write a script was powerful for a young girl.

When I studied dreams with Denise Linn, the author of *Hidden Power of Dreams,* in 2010, I finally found permission to trust myself to interpret my dreams. Over the years, I had read many books on dreams and found myself looking for the "right way" to interpret their messages. I sought validation for my intuition and the vibrant images I was seeing in the space between waking and sleeping. In the days of training with Denise, I discovered the power of trusting my own interpretations based on my associations and knowledge of the elements.

---

1 I created the term Twilight Threshold to help readers visualize the transitional point between day and night. I chose Twilight to describe the threshold as a place where the veil thins between two worlds, awake and dreaming. I describe the process of stepping into this transitional point of consciousness later in "Using this book" and more in Chapter 5.

With practice, I grew to appreciate the insights I captured in the imaginal realm so that I could move forward with a project, relationship or goal more freely. In fact, the study I did with dreams supported me to view the "dreaming" I did in my childhood as more practical than I had thought. In time, I started working with clients and inviting them into the imaginal realm for insight and guidance. I am interested in helping others to see the value of dreams and the imaginal realm so that they can work with this intuitive tool to enrich their lives. In turn, clients have been amazed at how easily messages flowed to them. This has inspired me to author a book that gives others a structure to connect with their inner realms of wisdom.

I offer *two avenues of dreamwork* for you in this book. One is to learn how to work with dreams in your sleep to gain insight into your everyday life. The other is to develop the skill to enter the imaginal realm from a waking state so that you can receive the intuitive wisdom that your rational mind may miss. Dreams and the Twilight Threshold, which I present later in this book, are especially powerful tools for steering your way through life's challenges.

In my experience, rational skills are readily taught and encouraged in society. The only person who will grant you permission to grow your intuitive skills is you. This book will help you feel more confident in your relationship with your inner mystic, so that you can take the next steps on this journey feeling more nourished and with greater clarity.

Using this book

There are things to keep in mind so that you can easily make the most of this book for your personal development.

First, be empowered to interpret for yourself the messages that you'll uncover with the processes laid out in this book. The unique significance of your dreams belongs only to you. Conversations with others may help to form your ideas and clarify what a dream means for you. Yet it is important to notice what resonates with you rather than what others see as the "true message." Give yourself permission to do this imperfectly and accept that some messages are more profound than others.

Second, be patient with yourself. *Trusting your imagination is vital* to the dream dialogue process and to your ability to linger in a dream state. Be willing to feel awkward discussing what you experience, and keep dropping back into the dream to notice all that you see, hear and feel. Give yourself permission to schedule time in the morning to practice the processes you're about to learn here. I suggest that you commit to 28 days of recording your dreams and accessing the Twilight Threshold, to develop a habit.

Third, although the four processes described in this book are easy, your logical mind usually gets in the way and starts to complicate things by overthinking. It is normal to doubt what we cannot see in the physical realm. For this reason, I also encourage you to practice with friends so that you can be helpers for each other when you enter the Twilight Threshold or return to a dream. When a professional or a friend holds the framework of these methods for you, you are free to step through the door to your dream and be present with what you find.

Here are some habits to help you recall dreams:

1. Put a journal or paper with a pen by your bed before you sleep.
2. Write a variant of the following affirmation on the paper and repeat silently before you go to sleep, "I nestle into my sleep and easily recall my dreams when I wake".
3. Jot down notes of what you dream as soon as you wake and before you move around in your bed. Moving your body tends to lift your mind out of the dream faster than you may think.
4. If you sense the dream lifting away from your grasp, roll back into the position you were last in when dreaming. For example, roll onto your right side or left side and see if the dream returns to you.

At the beginning of learning this process, it can help to train your mind to recall dreams by recording them when you wake in the night. Buy a pen that has a pinpoint light in it or use a flashlight to record your dream in the dark.

After reading this book, you will be able to do the following:

1. Choose a dreamwork method from this book to work on alone or with another person.
2. Revisit nightmares as a portal for spiritual growth.
3. Access a liminal state of mind to glean meaningful messages. In this book, I name this state of mind the Twilight Threshold.
4. Re-enter a dream state to create outcomes that empower you.

5. Have fun blending the mystical with the rational aspects of life!

This book introduces three methods to work with a dream:

1. Dream dialogue: a modification of a Gestalt model of dreamwork.
2. The movie director method, which invites you to re-enter a dream as if you're the movie director.
3. Symbolism: the symbolic language of elements of dreams to support your waking life.

This book also offers a method to access the imaginal realm from a waking state to allow for the possibilities that your conscious mind could not consider alone: Dropping into your Twilight Threshold, a liminal state of mind (a sensory threshold), to receive creative messages that you can bring to your waking life.

What is the Twilight Threshold?

For this book, I named the liminal space between awake and asleep the 'Twilight Threshold' because I want it to be easy for people to imagine this in-between state. Twilight is a point in time where the light suspends as the day and night transition. Light has a different quality for these few moments. Similarly, the mind experiences a transitional moment between awake and asleep.

In the Twilight Threshold, your mind's landscape has a softer, more mysterious focus. For many, you may experience a feeling of falling as you enter sleep. (Hence, the term "falling asleep.") This state of mind before you go to sleep (officially named hypnagogia) is detached from the waking reality and a powerful place to transform an area of your life that is stuck. For the purposes of my work, the intention in entering the

Twilight Threshold is to access the creative spark at the edge of your waking brain so that the doors of possibility open for you. You can also develop the capacity to enter the Twilight Threshold consciously, as shown in the upcoming chapters.

What is the Imaginal Realm?

The imaginal realm is a state of daydreaming where you can suspend rational thought and are open to receiving mysterious wisdom from beyond your own imagination.

What you experience in the imaginal realm may or may not be possible in the waking realm. For example, when you step into the imaginal realm, you may sense a deceased loved one inside a scene in your current life. If a message is not obvious, clarify the message later so that you continue to observe with your senses rather than words. Your mind and body experience the imaginal realm like a lived experience through sensations, images, smells and sounds.

The imaginal realm has a mystical quality because it is like entering an altered state of consciousness to gain support in life. You learn how to access the gifts of the imaginal realm using your breath or through a brief guided meditation in this book.

I encourage you to experiment with one or any combination of these four methods playfully and with curiosity. Take the pressure off and have some fun!

This book is not intended to be used to determine which dreams are precognitive, foretelling the future or telepathic.

CHAPTER ONE
LET US HAVE A LITTLE CONVERSATION WITH YOUR DREAM

"You be the kitten. I will be you," I say to Simone.

This sounds like a wacky technique to our literal minds. Yet, the dream dialogue technique is a powerful way to drop back into a dream for a message. In this chapter's sample dream process, I have a conversation with parts of Simone's dream so that you can see how Simone gains clues as to what the dream is telling her.

Simone is three months into a heavy journey that began when her mom was diagnosed with Alzheimer's. Her family recently moved her parents into assisted living, and they are in the process of selling her parent's home. By exploring a dream she has during this passage of life, Simone unlocks emotion related to her parent's mortality that is causing her to hold her breath and rush through her days. After working with her dream and having a conversation with aspects of her dream, she finds sadness, hope and playfulness.

Dreams offer hints for how you can restore inner balance in ways that you may not have considered in your waking life. When you examine a single moment of a dream, you create a little distance to view it differently. Then, you have a choice to consider how the scene from your dream relates to your waking life and how you may wish to respond to the perspective the dream dialogue has offered.

This chapter teaches you how to set up a dialogue between the Dreamer and an element of the dream (or the dreamworker and the Dreamer acting as a character in the dream) so that you're open to the possibility of a fresh perspective on the meaning of your dream. I teach you how to do a dream dialogue with a chart and script and then apply it to Simone's dream. You will learn how Simone's experience of the dream dialogue supports her to be more engaged with those she loves. Use this chapter as a guide to interpret messages with the dream dialogue method.

Before diving in, it may help to know that the dream dialogue process is based on Gestalt principles, which recognize that the mind instinctively perceives patterns and automatically puts pieces together to see the whole. When you interpret your dreams using this method, you look at the dream from the perspective of a character or other element of the dream. As you imagine being a single component in your dream, your mind begins to knit the pieces into a larger sense of your own life. The (Gestalt) dream dialogue is a powerful method to gain a holistic perspective of yourself and your situation.

How to do the dream dialogue method and use a chart

To make it easy to learn the process of dialoguing with a dream, I suggest that you create a chart. Years ago, I trained with Dr. Martha Beck, a Harvard-trained sociologist and founder of Wayfinder Life Coach training. She taught coaches a dream chart method that I use to this day. I adopted Dr. Beck's chart for this book and adjusted it to fit the method used here. The chart organizes the dialogue between the Dreamer and dream elements in a way that is easy to follow.

The first column is the element of the dream that the Dreamer wants to consider. The second column is the selected element's description of themselves. The third column is the element speaking to the Dreamer. *All columns are in first person to remind the Dreamer to become the part of the dream that they have chosen.*

I ask clients to select the elements of a dream that create a strong reaction when they recall the dream. Dream elements to consider can be anything that stands out in the dream, including a strong feeling, creatures, characters, the wind, the ocean, or even a color. Notice which elements of the dream increase your heart rate or raise the tone of your voice when you're retelling the dream. These subtle observations can help determine which parts of the dream to focus on first. It is not necessary to focus on all aspects of the dream. Sometimes all is revealed after one or two conversations with elements of a dream.

Inside the chart are questions to get a dialogue started with an element of the dream. The concept is to ask questions that prompt the Dreamer to step into the role of a particular aspect of the dream. Once the Dreamer steps into the role of the element, they speak in the present moment, as if all events in the dream are happening right now.

I strongly suggest using this process with a friend to help you step into character so that you can easily process insights from the dream. Therefore, I've set up the chart as though you have two people involved: you and your Dream Helper.

Of course, you could ask yourself these questions and interpret the dream on your own too. If you use this chart on your own to clarify a dream, then it may seem odd as you are the one asking and answering the questions. The key to working with a dream solo is to trust the process. Take a breath after you ask each question and let yourself return to the dream. Then, drop into the character and imagine the response of the element.

In this book, I act as the Dream Helper, and my name is used where a Dream Helper would be asking the question.

Tips to prepare for dialogue as a process:

- Notice that your logical mind may want to argue with "being" the element of the dream. It may feel awkward to say something like, "I am a book. I am wise, timeless and I have a message for Kirsten from her future." Go with it anyway. The process starts to flow quickly when you bring a playful curiosity.
- When working with dreams, the Dreamer must first get into a transitional, liminal space by taking some easy slow breaths to quieten and slow down.

An Example of Charting Dialogue

Choose and list elements of the dream.	Describe the element of the dream in first person and present tense.	Describe what the element sees and says to the Dreamer in first person and present tense.
For example, elements of the dream could be: - Red Shirt - Spider - Anxious Feeling - The Ocean	For example, Red Shirt says, "I am red, tight fitting and simple."	For example, Red Shirt says, "I am here to remind the Dreamer of how much she once loved the color red. She seems scared to stand out now. I want her to know it is safe to be bold."

Suggested prompts for the Dream Helper

The Dream Helper could ask these questions to help the Dreamer select elements of the dream:	Dream Helper could ask:	The Dream Helper could ask these questions to help the element speak in character:
"What part of the dream feels most intense?" "What aspect of the dream speaks to you loudest?" "Would you like to be that aspect?" Dream Helper could gently remind the Dreamer to embody their chosen element: "Great. So, now that you have chosen this element, remember that you are the element. Remember to speak in the first person. For example, I am the _____ [insert element of the dream]." After the Dreamer has stepped into the selected parts of the dream and the process is complete, ask: "What overall message do you think this dream has for you?"	"How would you describe yourself, Red Shirt [or insert element of dream]?" When, and if, the Dreamer slips up and says, for example, "He is bright and scary," the Dream Helper should kindly remind the Dreamer to be the element and speak in the first person. For example, "I am red and a little scary to others who see me."	"What do you see and feel?" "Why are you in the dream? Do you have a purpose?" "What do you want?" "What do you have to say to the Dreamer?" "Do you have a message for the Dreamer?" **A helpful last question:** "Is there any last thing you want to say?"

Transitioning between different elements of a dream

In between elements of the dream, it is helpful for the Dream Helper (or yourself if you are working alone) to say to the element: "Thank you, ____ [element of dream], for showing up and sharing this with [me/the Dreamer]."

Then I suggest the Dream Helper prompts the Dreamer to take some deep breaths and imagine standing under a waterfall to clear the connection with the element of the dream. The process of imagining a waterfall is intended to clear any emotion or sensations that transpire in the process of stepping into the role of the dream element. Using a visualization like a waterfall helps to clear the Dreamer's focus between dream elements.

Simone's dream – the dream dialogue chart and script in action

First, I ask Simone to summarize her dream. Some people have epic dreams that could be written as a trilogy and others only recall snippets. If the Dreamer starts to get lost in the detail of a long dream saga, I suggest you ask them to summarize the key points that stand out most to them.

In Simone's dream, she finds herself in the basement of her childhood home with kittens that are multiplying before her eyes. She feels overwhelmed, wondering how to get rid of the kittens. Each time she looks away, more kittens return. Eventually, she walks upstairs to find her mom cooking a turkey in the oven. There is a knock on the door and Simone opens the door to someone who says they are the new owner of the home, and they are angry. Simone tries to get rid of the new owner and tells her parents, "We have to leave!" She feels a strong urgency to get out of the house.

Let us have a little conversation with your dream

Second, I begin a conversation with Simone by asking her to *become elements of the dream*. I explain that she may discover a different attitude when she steps into the shoes of the characters. For instance, I ask Simone to be one of the kittens, and she then describes herself as alone, skinny and meek. Then, I ask Simone to speak to me as if she is one of the kittens and tell me what is happening through their eyes. I take down notes to help Simone remember later what she said, but most often in these conversations, the Dreamer, like Simone, starts to feel things shift in themselves straight away. Often the Dreamer starts to immediately process something they could not have seen without the dream conversation.

The chart below shows how I set up Simone to be parts of her dream. I take the role of Dream Helper and prompt her with relevant questions (see previous chart), making note of what she says. Later in the chapter, I show how our conversation continued, to demonstrate how a dialogue transitions into insights that support waking life. The discussion after the dialogue also explores symbolic messages in reference to the kittens.

Simone's Chart

Element of the dream	Describe yourself as this element.	What is happening through your eyes? What message do you have for Simone?
Kittens	I look like loaves of bread. I keep multiplying. I am scared, alone, skinny, meek.	I am little and this basement feels so big. If there were carpet, I would not be so cold. I need to be taken care of. Your mom is feeling scared, alone and meek, like me. I want you to see that she is not alone and that is why she [Simone] keeps finding more of us.
The Oven	I am present, aware, and I get to see things others do not see.	Your mom is capable and carefree. There is no lack of time – no sense of urgency. I feel warm and full. You cannot be aware of everything.

Let us have a little conversation with your dream 17

Element of the dream	Describe yourself as this element.	What is happening through your eyes? What message do you have for Simone?
The Voice of Urgency. "We have to leave."	I am prickly, rapid, urgent. NOTE: The Voice of Urgency speaks in a tone that is authoritarian, hurried and rigid. *Kirsten says to the Voice of Urgency: What happens if you took down your guard and were less urgent?*	I am everywhere in your waking life. I am the feeling of being stuck in purgatory and being unable to finish tasks. I remind people to get things done. I am the noise in your head that says, "Be done selling the house. Be done with childhood. Be done pulling up everything from the past." It would hurt too much. And it would be too painful and too sad for you.
	Kirsten says to Voice of Urgency: What message do you have underneath this pain and urgency?	Simone, you do not have to hurry. Be patient.

Follow-up questions and moving beyond the chart

As you skim the chart, you may find that some of the responses do not make sense to you. Remember that it is the Dreamer who gains insight through this process. The Dream Helper is welcome to ask clarifying questions so that the Dreamer gets more value from the dialogue, but they do not interpret the dream. *The Dreamer is meant to stay in character until the element has said all it wants to say. The Dreamer should speak in first person as if they are the dream element.*

In this example with Simone, it is worth explaining that when Simone stepped into the character of the "Voice of Urgency," she became very charged. *If you are helping someone with their dream, and you notice there is a charge in the Dreamer's voice, then you have found a clue to explore the dialogue a little more.* In this case, when the element brings a charge to the conversation, it is difficult to get helpful insight. This is no different from when we are defensive or mad in our waking life and can't access our most intelligent thinking. There is room in the dream dialogue to ask questions other than those I suggest in the prompts, so that you may interact creatively with the characters of the dream. I invited Simone to dig deeper into this element of the dream by asking her some questions that required her to speak as the "Voice of Urgency" and explain its motivations. When Simone was embodying the Voice of Urgency, I asked her two follow-up questions after the ones you see in the chart:

> Kirsten: What would happen if you took down your guard and were less urgent?
>
> Simone as the Voice of Urgency: Then it would hurt too much. It would be too painful and too sad for Simone.
>
> Kirsten: What is underneath this pain and urgency?
>
> Simone as the Voice of Urgency: Simone, you do not have to hurry. Be patient.

Initially, Simone answered my question as the Voice of Urgency and spoke in a demanding, rushed tone. When I invited Voice of Urgency to take down its guard, Simone discovered a gift. The Voice of Urgency had been protecting Simone from feeling sad, but through the dialogue, the voice became an advocate for patience with herself and her family. Underneath all the rushing was an urge to protect the love she had for her parents.

The dream dialogue process is meant to be fluid and if it seems like the best thing to do is pause and take a breath to reset, then it is best to do that. In addition, if the Dreamer finds she wants to ask a question of the "element" in the dream, she can do so and then step back into being the "element." When you are in this process, you may notice that you simply hear a message speaking to you. You will see an example of how fluid this becomes in future chapters. The dream chart is meant to be like a map that prompts you to navigate the imaginal realm until it becomes apparent that you don't need the map anymore.

Bear in mind that it doesn't matter if the chart is filled out "correctly". It is your openness to the process that allows you to step through to meet the wisdom of your mystical mind. The key points in the process to return to are 1.) step into first person and be part of the dream and 2.) speak in the present tense. At the end of the dream dialogue process, the Dreamer will have determined the meaning of the dream for themself.

Questions, symbols and writing prompts to clarify a message and take action

The dream dialogue chart allows the mind to begin unifying the parts of the dream into a whole message. The next steps here amplify the message by making it actionable in the waking world. You can use an adaptation of the questions I used with Simone, along with the symbolism suggestions and writing prompts below. Symbolism and writing prompts help you to get more specific so that the meaning is even more applicable.

After completing the dialogue process, I asked Simone how she viewed the dream now, which is a question to ask yourself or the Dreamer every time you finish the dream dialogue chart. In reflection, she summarized, "This has been a long couple of months. My dream points out that I am getting impatient and that it is not helpful to rush my feelings or the end-of-life process. The dream dialogue has given me a reminder to be open and patient even when it is hard."

At this point, I reviewed the chart and observed that her dream had kittens, not cats. I wondered what the symbolism of kittens could be. *It is helpful to be curious about the description of the dream so that you can open your mind to further insight.* Symbolism can first be found by asking the Dreamer what associations they have with the element. After this, you could also jump to a dream or symbol dictionary by using Google if you want to explore other views on symbolic meaning. The most potent meaning is the one that resonates most with the Dreamer, as you will see in the upcoming chapter with Celia.

When you want to explore elements of the dream and their symbolic message, you can use a version of the dialogue here. I have captured part of the conversation with Simone to help you get a sense of how that may work:

> Kirsten: What qualities do you relate to kittens more than cats and other animals?
>
> Simone: They are playful. They get into trouble. They get into stuff. They get lost. Cats are careful, but kittens are playful and curious.
>
> K: Perhaps then the kittens are suggesting that you bring a little playfulness into your life. A kitten needs a safe place. It is not yet a cat and may get into trouble, so perhaps set up a safe structure for yourself. How does this land with you as another message in the dream?
>
> S: In general, being playful is outside my comfort zone. I am a planner and would have to think about being playful. I would have to choose something carefully [laughs].

Let us have a little conversation with your dream

Kirsten: Could you approach dinner or a phone call in a way that's a little more kitten-like or playful?

S: Yes, that fits.

K: What will you take away from this dream?

S: I will take away the timelessness part. This is not something to rush. It is not something I can work toward. Most of the things I have gone after have been goals. This is not a goal I want to get to – to get through this is death, so, I do not want to rush that. Now I have some ideas on how to be during this time. I could be different – open, patient and playful. Later Simone summarized the takeaway for her.

S: The dream is preparation for the next phase of connecting with my mom. This dream is helping me to be more present and to choose to cultivate more playfulness with myself. And more openness. [Simone smiles and laughs.]

If this is your dream, take a moment to journal your reflections on the process. Here are some suggestions for writing prompts:

1. What stood out to you in the dialogue when you became the characters in the dream?
2. Write about what you will do differently now that you have gained these perspectives.
3. What do you notice in your body after doing the process with the dream dialogue? For instance, have your shoulders dropped? Has your chest softened? Notice and name an awareness of tension or relaxation in 1-3 areas of your body.

The act of writing gives palpable shape to the intangible shifts you experienced. Furthermore, when you make the time to write down: 1.) the observations of your physical experience and 2.) the impact the process will have on your behavior, you authenticate this dream process for yourself. By writing down these impressions, you acknowledge and value your inner mystic, while putting your insights into a form your rational mind can use. Repeating this last step in the process by writing down your observations strengthens the relationship between your intuition and your logical mind.

How the dreamwork impacted Simone in the days ahead

I followed up with Simone a week after our conversation with her dream. She said that she had been more aware of moments to let go of urgency and laugh off some of the heaviness. Following our session, she had dreams of her parents trying to move back into their house. She thought, "You can't stay here." However, she then laughed and *was able to see the joy her parents felt inside the dream instead of quickly moving them on.*

A week later, Simone sent an email to me with photos of her current home. She had redone a wall in her bathroom with photos of her kids laughing and a frame with the statement, "Let that shit go." Simone reported that the wall invited more playfulness in her daily life as she laughs every time she sees the framed photos.

Simone's dream dialogue demonstrates that slowing down to pay attention to your dreams is a valuable way to support yourself during stressful times in your life. This dream gave Simone the gift of accessing how her heart wanted to connect with her parents in this last act of their life. Unwrapping her dream's message helped Simone to support herself differently in her waking life so that she felt more present with those she loves.

CHAPTER TWO
GET IN THE DRIVER'S SEAT WITH YOUR NIGHTMARE

Most dreams are your brain's attempt to process memories or stressful circumstances in your life. The dream dialogue awakens your ability to insert free will into that dream. The *process reminds you that you are the author of the dream as well as a character in the dream, which empowers you to recall that you have a choice in how you behave.* Recollect that after her dreamwork session with me, Simone *could hear herself think in her dream*. She said, "You can't stay here," when her parents wanted to return to their house. Then, she chose to lighten up and laugh instead of rushing her parents, both in the dream and in her waking life.

In this chapter, I show how nightmares are a magic portal, where you can activate your personal authority and transform your perspective in your waking life. I view nightmares as especially potent dreams to interact with, due to the charge they hold in your body. If you have heard someone whimper or breathe quickly in their sleep, then you know the physical effect dreams can have on you. Likewise, addressing a nightmare allows you to bring change into your material world. A nightmare can also be your soul calling out to you, "Wake up to this moment in your life." If not acknowledged, you can feel sucked into the powerlessness of the dream, and you may miss the gift that is waiting for you.

I believe that nightmares can be a version of rumination. Rumination means getting caught in a loop of negative thoughts which cause distress and intrude on the healthy function of your daily life. Both nightmares and rumination feed on incessant thoughts that tell you that you have no choice in a situation. Learning how to work with nightmares helps you climb out of the automatic responses to fear so that you stop feeling trapped or defensive, and instead, learn helpful ways to work with fear in your day-to-day life. In fact, nightmares are wonderful places to train yourself to remember what is in your control when life feels out of control.

In this chapter's dream example, I work with Celia, my daughter, who has a nightmare that is so vivid she can feel it in her mind and body for two days afterwards. Through re-imagining the nightmare, the seat of control is returned to her, and a sense of equilibrium is restored to her mind and body.

It is common to have dreams of death at distinct stages of growth, such as when moving into adulthood. The techniques here also illustrate how a parent may support a child or young adult with "bad" dreams so that they can reclaim a sense of their own personal agency. Remember that humans, like all living creatures, grow through periods of stress. For example, growing pains in your knees as a kid indicate the growth of the body. Likewise, the stress of a nightmare is like a smoke signal for personal and spiritual growth.

Revisit a nightmare to restore your sense of control, even in fearful moments

When she has this nightmare, Celia is 17 years old and in her last month of high school. In Celia's dream, she is at work, sitting down in a group meeting, and she sees spiders on the wall, which terrify her. She looks down and is startled to see a spider on her elbow and another one on her hand. The spiders bite her with their massive fangs. She screams for help. Her friend gets the spider off her hand, but the fangs stay in her skin. When she shakes her hand, the fangs fall off, but holes remain. The manager takes the spider off her elbow and kills it.

The dream transmutes to a second part...

Celia is in a narrow hallway with all sorts of doors. Each time she opens a door there is a dog in a different scene, like a different house and yard. One dog says, "I want to come out. I want to grow old. I want to grow up." So, Celia opens the doors and lets the dogs out into the hallway. They start aging rapidly, from puppies to dying old dogs. She is upset because she does not want them to die. She tries to get the dogs back in their doors to make them young again, but the doors have changed, and she cannot make them young again. One door is a storage unit door and is very creepy. She opens it. There is a woman standing in the door with a clear bag over her like a mummy. Celia wakes in fear.

After Celia tells me her dream, I ask Celia to imagine that she is one of the elements of her dream. As seen in the previous chapter, this is a useful way of understanding a dream. Celia stepped into the character of a spider, like Simone did with the kitten.

I walked Celia through the dream dialogue process with the spider because the spider was by far the most charged element of the first half of her dream. Celia went from being scared and confused to gaining personal insight as she described the dream to me. By stepping fully into the character of the spider, she could see that the spider represented her childhood fears and that it was time to reconsider how she lashed out quickly when she was scared or upset.

After the dialogue with the spider, I invite Celia to close her eyes, return to the dream and imagine that she has a support team with her in the dream this time. This is the movie director method, which I will outline in Chapter 4. Celia discovers some sadness that she is suppressing in her waking life, sheds tears and commences a different relationship with this stage of her life. She realizes her feelings of loss and fear are around getting older.

The movie director method invites you to get back into the driver's seat of a dream. It can be tricky with nightmares to feel like you have any control at all. Consequently, it is especially helpful to imagine real-world and spiritual allies to join you as you re-enter the dream so that you feel encouraged to be brave. This method allows Celia to remember her own inner resources as she re-imagines the dream. Celia's experience of working with parts of her nightmare and then reconceiving it, details how a nightmare can become a valued counselor on your soul's journey.

Revisiting nightmares is like returning a light sword to the hero who is being attacked by monsters. When you wake from a bad dream, you too can return to the dream and insert your superpowers into the scenes so that you don't let the dream end with a sense of being helpless or a victim. What you can shift in the night spills over into your mindset and the actions you take in the day.

Using the dream dialogue and movie director method with Celia's nightmare

You can further understand how to use the dream dialogue technique and the movie director method by reading my notes on the process with Celia.

First, we dialogued with the dream, as seen by following the chart. I started by asking Celia to become an element or character in her dream. She chose the spider and her responses as the spider are in the middle and right columns.

Notice the progression of insight as we dialogue between the spider, Celia and me. Celia jumps in with personal insight, as you will see further on, where I record Celia speaking as herself in the chart. This insight by Celia shown in the chart demonstrates how fluid this process can become. If possible, get a friend to help by asking questions that prompt you to be the element of the dream. This allows you to drop more fully into being the character or element of the nightmare.

Celia's Chart

Element of dream: Spider	Describe yourself as the element.	My message for Celia or what I want to say
Spider:	I feel small. I am scared. I am ugly.	"She (Celia) fears spiders and bugs. I was giving her a fright because she has little girl fears, and she is meant to be growing up. Those fangs were snapped off."
Celia jumps in and speaks as herself:	The spider is a metaphor for all my fears and that I should get over them.	
Kirsten asks Spider:	Why did you bite Celia?	I was scared.
Celia:	The spider is like me. When I feel nervous or not in control, I get scared and lash out and hurt someone. I feel regret after I lash out. The spider reminds me of how I behave with a childhood fear: I lash out and leave the room when I am scared or upset.	

Recall that in Chapter 1 I invited you to dig deeper into conversation with a part of the dream with questions in freeform. I was curious why the spider bit Celia, so I asked, "Why did you bite Celia?" Celia jumped in and replied, "The spider is like me. When I feel nervous or not in control, I get scared and lash out and hurt someone. I feel regret after I lash out. The spider reminds me of how I behave with a childhood fear: I lash out and leave the room when I am scared or upset."

After doing the dream dialogue with the spider, I encouraged Celia **to re-imagine how the dream would go if:**

1. she could influence what happens in the dream, and
2. she brought along a support team when she re-entered the dream.

I recount the conversation with Celia below so that you can get another sense of what it looks like to do movie direction for a dream. Notice what happens as Celia re-imagines the dream. The process stings her heart in such a way that she immediately relates it to a current sadness in her life. (See Chapter 4 on the movie director technique for additional details on the process).

> Kirsten: Relax and breathe and soften into the dream again. However, this time re-enter the dream and imagine that you are with your allies. You can invite anyone to come into the dream who helps you feel like the hero of this dream. You are the movie director of this dream and can change how the scenes unfold in the dream.
>
> Celia: [Her eyes are closed, and she is relaxed on the couch]. The spider does not bite me. When I see the spider on me, it spins a web and drops to the floor. I do not kill it. I am slightly scared and then I let the spider go. The others in the room at work do not even notice. I deal with the spider calmly. The spider goes on the ground and back to the web and I leave the room without paying it much attention. I do not feel as scared.

Before I can lead Celia to re-imagine the second segment of the dream, she has a self-realization:

C: I want to grow up and leave childhood, but I also worry about time passing by and getting old. There are people younger than me now. And it is my time to grow up. When I opened the door [in the dream] it was all black and only a person was there. I feared dying, everyone dying. I really get it now: once you are out of childhood, you cannot go back.

K: Now how do you feel?

C: Sad. [Covers her face and cries.]

After a pause, I invite Celia to re-imagine the second part of her dream with a support team again at her side. This act of bringing a support team into the dream brings her courage.

C: I open the doors and see different scenes playing out inside each door. When it is time for the dogs to come out and age in the hallway, I see them playing. It is not so sad. They age slower. When they get old and are dying, they are there to support each other. It is not a sad thing. It is like a content feeling. And the door with the scary person never opens.

K: Who did you imagine was beside you in the dream when you re-entered the hallway?

C: [Crying] I had you and Lucy [our pet dog in waking life].

K: I can understand what you are saying. This time in your life is like being between two worlds. Something is dying, like your childhood, or not relating to me as your mom, like you used to. Yet, you are not fully in adulthood. You still live at home. It is a time to let go for the next stage to be born. It can feel scary, and it is going to be okay.

While this dream was also ripe with symbolism around the meaning of dogs and spiders, Celia felt complete with her process by the time we finished re-imagining her nightmare. However, she did mention later that more dog dreams (not nightmares) followed our dream session together.

Celia looked up dog symbolism on Google. She decided that the dogs were acting as guardians in her dreams and protecting her, which reframed her dreams in a more positive light. While there is value in using a dictionary to generate ideas on what a symbol could mean, it is important that you stay centered in your personal experience to determine what a symbol could mean for you. In the case of dreams and the imaginal realm, the value is noticing which part of a definition connects with you. This process of using a reference to inspire insight is what Celia did when she noticed dogs repeating in her dreams.

Notice that Celia, like Simone, experiences a shift as she walks through the techniques. The dream was not purely symbolic with a message to interpret "correctly." Instead, the dream offered up a soup of information that was waiting to be digested with her mind, creativity and intuition. The intention of re-entering a dream is to return to a sense of your own personal agency and to remember that you have the capacity to choose what happens in a dream and in real life. *Once you begin to re-imagine your dream, the inner shift becomes possible in the physical realm too.*

Unwrapping the gifts of Celia's nightmare opened Celia's grief for the loss of a protected stage of childhood. In turn, she transformed her fear and found some peace with the reality of stepping into adulthood. In fact, she found ways to creatively support herself through one of life's most significant passages.

CHAPTER THREE
THE TINIEST FRAGMENT OF A DREAM CAN SPEAK VOLUMES

A tiny fragment of a dream can be loaded with the potential to transform us. If you do not recall much of your dream, this brief chapter will show you how you can still use dialogue to gain a message and a shift in awareness. This chapter's dream sample also portrays a dialogue with a *feeling*. Though Sofia's dream recollection is short, her feeling of fearless joy as she bungee jumps is *unusually* intense, which is worth exploring further because heights create fear in her waking life. This delightful fragment of a dream transforms Sofia's relationship with falling and flying.

Prior to our dreamwork session, I asked Sofia what her mood was on a scale of 1–10 (with 10 being high). She felt about a 5, and she was feeling tired. In a short space of time, Sofia shifted to feeling more energy (7 out of 10) and found an unexpectedly helpful message with clear instructions on how to find more joy every day. Sofia's quick conversation with a part of her dream is also a testament to how a fragment of a dream can be a brief, potent way to bring about a shift in your energy. You do not need substantial amounts of time to support yourself in this journey with your dreams or the imaginal realm.

In Sofia's dream, she is at a theme park that has bungee jumping. She surprises everyone when she does the bungee jump because she is usually fearful of heights. In her dream, she recalls a powerful sense that she will not die. In fact, she feels pure joy when she jumps. There is also a brave, younger girl in the dream, Dahlia, and she reminds Sofia of when she, too, was youthful and brave.

When I asked Sofia to be the Fearless Joy in her dream, Sofia easily slipped into character. Fearless Joy became animated and easily talked to Sofia in the manner of a fun, grandmotherly character. She told Sofia that fear was taking up too much space in her life and reminded Sofia that there used to be more room for joy in her younger life!

Since the process was so easy for Sofia, I carried the conversation further than the usual dream dialogue and supported Sofia to connect with the wisdom of Fearless Joy. In this session, she enters the liminal space of the Twilight Threshold (how to do so is discussed further in Chapter 5) and she gets instructions for how she can personally land more joy within micro-moments in her daily life, which you can read more about below.

Sofia's Chart

Symbolic element	Describe yourself as the element	What do you see in this scene or dream? What message do you have for Sofia?
Fearless Joy	I am like Sofia used to be when she was a little girl. Super brave and fearless; I am amplified. Big. Blissful. Amazing and free.	There is more room for me, Joy, if she would shoo away the fear. (She makes a hand gesture like shooing a fly.) Fear is taking up too much space in her life. Her fear of death is everywhere. The little girl in this dream, Dahlia, reminds me that I used to have more room in Sofia's life.

A script of the dialogue with Sofia's dream — discover specific guidance for your life

Sofia was excited about this feeling of fearless joy she found in her dream. Based on her interest, I carried the conversation further with Sofia after we filled out the dream chart. You can use these *questions, or modify them, when you want to expand on something that gets your attention in your dreams.*

Sofia: I want to thank the Fearless Joy. I want to know how to feel more fearless joy.

Kirsten: Okay, let us drop into the element [Fearless Joy]. Be Joy. Close your eyes. Slow down your breath. [*Sofia takes a moment*]. What do you hear?

S: That Fearless Joy is always here. It is my choice to tap into it.

K: Anything else?

S: I love Fearless Joy so much. I want more of this.

K: Stay with [Joy] and befriend it. Make a commitment to each other. How will you show up for Joy and make room for them? How will Joy be here for you?

I will be silent while you go inside yourself and be with Joy. Stay with Joy for as long as you wish, and then, come back to me and share when you are ready.

[I allow a quiet pause in conversation.]

S: So, the message is clear. The fear is in my head. The joy is in my heart. I need to move into my heart.

K: Are you willing to do that?

S: Yes.

K: Do you know how to do that? Or do you want to go inside and ask Joy how you might do that?

[Silence as Sofia again closes her eyes.]

S: Joy is telling me to ground myself and be more present because it is always there.

K: Ask Joy what it would look like to be grounded more often. Ask for specifics.

[Silence as Sofia again closes her eyes to connect with Joy.]

S: [*With eyes still closed*] Joy has told me to have little micro-moments. When doing the routine things that I do every day, like brushing my teeth or walking out the front gate, I am to make little moments for myself. Moments in which I choose to be present. It does not take long. Maybe a few deep breaths to allow me to be in the present moment throughout my day, like washing the dishes mindfully.

K: Taking moments to be present. If you do that, joy will come.

S: *[Opens eyes and speaks with enthusiasm.]* Joy is saying it is always there. It is about my tapping into it.

The day after our session, Sofia messaged me to share that she had flown on a plane. She excitedly reported, "I normally would be scared during takeoff and landing, but this time I consciously chose joy. It was like there was no room for fear when joy was there, like you cannot do both at the same time. The fear instantly disappeared, as in my dream. Joy was a big bubble that took up all the room and shoved fear out of the way. This is so amazing!"

When Sofia unwrapped the messages from her dream fragment, she transformed her relationship with flying and falling into the unknown, into something positive, which was made possible by slowing down to dialogue with the element of her dream. We never know exactly what a dream may be telling us unless we take the time to explore it with intuitive skills that are available to all of us. Remember that there is no "right" message to find in your dreams. *It is your openness to the dream process and the imaginal realm that allows you to glean insight.*

CHAPTER FOUR
BECOME THE MOVIE DIRECTOR OF YOUR LIFE AND DREAMS

When you wake in your sleep and deliberately rehearse a better outcome for a dream or a real-life scenario, you build confidence in your ability to guide your life. Somewhere on the brink of being awake and asleep, you have the power to rewire your brain and affirm yourself as the hero (as opposed to the victim) of your life. Celia discovered her ability to assert her authority when she re-entered her nightmare and purposefully let the spider spin a web and drop to the floor, rather than getting swept away with her fear of spiders and feeling powerless to a spider bite. This chapter outlines the movie director method, which you can use to shepherd solutions for waking life challenges and to take command of dreams when asleep.

When you apply the movie director method in the Twilight Threshold, insights, inner shifts, and guidance flow to you. This technique taps into the intelligence of your intuition. Whether or not your intuition is "right" does not matter. It is your openness to experiment with what comes to you that makes the difference. Redirect a dream or challenging situation with a curiosity for the images, words and feelings you sense. Rinse and repeat the process until you resonate with what you visualize. Then, create a logical way to evaluate and implement what you envision.

To help you understand the power of using the movie director method in real-life situations, I share a session I had with Shyla. Shyla wanted to feel more at ease with Nina, a woman in her social circles. It had come to the stage where Shyla felt dread when she saw Nina's car parked outside an event. Nina was unhappy in her marriage and spent a lot of time visiting friends. Consequently, Shyla hardly ever caught her other friends alone because they were so often with Nina. Shyla also admitted that she judged Nina for spending too much time visiting friends' houses and not trying harder in her marriage.

Shyla intended to use the dreamwork session with me so that she could find a way to be more accepting and flexible with Nina at dinners and gatherings. I chose to use the power of the Twilight Threshold because the mind is more malleable in this state, which would allow Shyla to detect and interact with her intuition for the inner shifts she desired. I began by guiding Shyla to a relaxed state of mind so that she could easily enter the Twilight Threshold.

Once she felt her mind was centered in the uninhibited state of the imaginal realm, Shyla returned to an old scene from her memory and imagined that she greeted Nina at her car outside their mutual friend's house. From this point on, Shyla began to observe her intuition and be open to what could happen. She visualized a conversation with Nina and silently asked Nina what she wanted. Nina gently told her that she wanted space to be herself and to deal with her challenges her own way. Almost immediately, I witnessed Shyla's whole body soften. She said that she felt a calm wash over her body and a sense of harmony with life. I include the script below so that you can see the process.

Navigate waking life situations with more clarity and compassion — use the movie director method

The questions I ask Shyla could be modified to suit your situation or for a Dream Helper to use with you.

> Kirsten: I would like you now to go to the incident that feels the strongest in your recent memory. Is it the scene where you drove up and saw her car? Pick an experience that was recently in your waking world.
>
> [*Pause*] Have you picked a scene?
>
> Before we begin, bring into this space allies or helpers for support as you re-imagine the scene. Remember a helper can be a loved one that has passed over, a spirit animal, someone you admire, or a general sense of your ancestors.
>
> Nod when you are ready.
>
> We will work with the scene as if it were a movie. You will direct the movie to play out however you wish.
>
> As the movie unfolds, you will get a chance to navigate through the scene. I would like you to dialogue with Nina. Ask your allies or guides for help at any time.
>
> Ask Nina a question. [*Pause*] Now, I would like you to become Nina and respond. If you do not know what she is saying, be patient. Trust your imagination to know. If needed, ask your allies to help you find compassionate words to say to Nina. Remember, you are the director.
>
> I will be silent for a bit to allow you to have a chance to feel as if you are truly in the movie, to connect with Nina, to become Nina, and to dialogue with Nina. You can come back to me for help at any time.
>
> [*Silence passes while Shyla slips into her imagination.*]
>
> How is the movie going? Need more time?

Shyla: No, I am good.

K: What is the overall message you want to take away from your movie?

S: She needs this [all the extra time with friends]. She really needs this. And she is asking for some space. And she is still listening. She is still watching. But she just needs this. I can totally give it to her.

K: That's Nina you reference as needing space?

S: Yeah.

K: What's the message for you? What do you feel?

S: It is a hard one to describe. Um, I feel more like myself.

K: What's it like being more like you?

S: It is like a humming feeling. Harmonious. You know when you are in the bush [forest], and you can just hear the bush. It is like that. Like a symphony that you cannot hear unless you are listening.

Although it may seem fake to use your imagination with a real-life situation, *the body and mind do not distinguish between real and unreal in this soft state of mind.* In this example, Shyla felt serenity in her body as the dialogue evolved, in the same way that you may cry at the cinema watching a sad scene. When you redirect a scene in your life, your body and mind come along with you. You seed a shift in your heart.

When Shyla was in the Twilight Threshold and connected with Nina, she was able to feel empathy with Nina, which brought a feeling of peace in her body and mind. Shyla spontaneously recognized that she was not taking time to nourish her spirit in her own life. She then realized that her own lack of self-care was why she was annoyed with Nina for taking lots of time for herself, away from her husband.

As a result of the movie direction method, Shyla decided that the whole experience with Nina in the imaginal realm was a message to reclaim activities that brought her own sense of harmony. She made a commitment at the end of our session to join a yoga class and explore other options to nurture her interests.

Months later I followed up with Shyla to learn how and if the exercise had made a lasting impact on her day-to-day life. The one conversation in the imaginal realm with Nina had shifted her so powerfully that she had forgotten how annoyed she had been with Nina and herself. In fact, she had built self-care practices, like swimming and pottery, back into her regular schedule. She was no longer annoyed with Nina and had happily stepped back from the friendship. She laughed to realize that she had given Nina the space she asked for in the imaginal realm and that it all had worked out.

When Shyla utilized the movie director method, she crossed over into a realm that allowed her to uncover a new way to respond to an impasse with another person. Using her intuition in the Twilight Threshold, she sensed another way to perceive her friend and returned to a more flexible way of responding to Nina.

Shyla's transformation is a testament to the far-reaching wisdom and creativity available to you in the imaginal realm. This process was equally powerful for Celia when she re-imagined her nightmare. For Celia, instead of healing an impasse, the process allowed her to have more compassion for herself as she crossed the threshold into adulthood.

How to use the movie director method

In the movie director method, you direct the movie *and* star in the movie. Because you remain tethered to your inner authority inside the imaginal realm, you have the choice to go back and edit how other characters respond to you and how you treat them. In this way, the movie director method uses the plasticity of imagination and builds on the concept of the dream dialogue that you have seen in previous chapters.

The movie director method usually includes:

- relaxing into the *Twilight Threshold*
- re-imagining a situation
- dialoguing with characters from a situation in life (or with the dream elements, as in previous chapters)
- returning to the wakeful realm to notice and evaluate the experience.

For the movie director method to be effective, you need to be fully relaxed. Breathe slowly and easily, and allow yourself to become soft and trusting before movie directing. With stress in the body, the mind wants to only focus on the problem(s) in front of us. We can have difficulty allowing our imagination to be fluid when pressured. Therefore, it can be helpful to acknowledge any difficult thoughts and feelings that come up. By acknowledging your discomfort, your mind will not feel the need to fight relaxation.

If you have difficulty entering your Twilight Threshold, I offer a free guided meditation (https://kb.kirstenbridge.com/book-downloads) to help you slow down and enter this soft and open state of mind where your conscious mind is in the background.

When in the Twilight Threshold, bring a frustrating situation to mind. Notice a strong emotion may start to draw you away from the imaginal realm. Breathe. Once you are in the open, softer state of mind, ask a character in your situation a question. Observe the dialogue. Notice what wants to happen and try playing out what you sense could be possible.

As director, you can enter your personal will into the scene and change the ending. You can take anything from the past and transform it in your imagination. This process opens doorways of potential in the waking world. If you imagine it, you open a gateway that alters your waking life.

Ask for help from your spiritual allies (mentors, loved ones who've passed over, angels, historical figures, animals, ancestors), as Celia did in Chapter 2. You may imagine one helper in the imaginal realm standing by your side or many near you. Trust who comes to your imagination when you ask helpers to come to your side. *When you sense that you have the support of a personal team, you ignite the values in your heart that are aligned with your highest vision of yourself.* Re-entering a tricky situation, or a dream, with the sense of helpers at your back often brings forward courage and curiosity.

IMPORTANT NOTE: If your issue is related to some form of trauma, I do not recommend you do this on your own. I suggest you work with a professional counselor so that you do not re-trigger yourself. This exercise is intended for current situations that frustrate you and for patterned responses to people that are no longer bringing you joy.

CHAPTER 5
TAKE IT FURTHER AND ENTER THE TWILIGHT THRESHOLD ON YOUR OWN

Of any method in this book, training your mind to enter the Twilight Threshold is the most powerful technique to use on your own for problem-solving and personal support. Creativity and insights come to you when your mind is in this transitional state.

Training yourself to navigate the Twilight Threshold unlocks doorways that lead to insight waiting for you. I offer a personal experience here to demonstrate how you can use the mornings as you wake to slide into the Twilight Threshold and dialogue with the imaginal realm.

One morning, as I began to emerge from a deep sleep, my anxiety related to drafting this book began to creep into my consciousness. I wanted to unhook from my anxiety over finishing the book so that I could stay the course of my vision to get it into the world. I knew my imagination was most creative and open in the Twilight Threshold, which occurs just before waking. So, I decided to linger in bed longer than usual to explore what I could access in the imaginal realm to help me finish this writing stage.

I silently asked, "How can I move forward to finish this book more easily? Can I see this book being done?"

At once, I saw an image of me sitting at my desk working on my book. The image stirred up feelings of frustration. I knew the intensity of the frustration could jolt me into a fully awake state if I stayed in this scene in my imagination. So, I used my rational mind to direct myself to try again, noting that this image was not an answer to my question. I rolled over to my other side and hugged my pillow. I began to soften back into the gap before sleep, to accept answers to my questions.

Instantly, I saw the book become an animated character. Little stars were moving around the book. The sound of its voice suggested a feminine character. Here is what I heard in the imaginal realm:

> Book: I really want to be written. Thank you for being the author.
>
> Kirsten: Wow, you are thanking me?
>
> Book: Yes! You are meant to be writing me. I want to be written, and I am so glad that it is you.

What a delightful surprise and new perspective to add some fun to finish this book. Through this liminal experience with my unfinished book, I felt renewed and encouraged. In fact, I felt a connection with something greater than me, like I was part of a team. Though I was directing the dialogue, Book's words came from the imaginal realm, from beyond my consciousness. Not only did Book's words surprise me, but I was also struck with wonder by the image of the animated stars surrounding the book as it spoke. I could feel the book's gratitude that I was bringing her into the world, and I was surprised to sense the paralyzing pressure to complete the book lift. Instead, I felt a playfulness towards writing this book.

I found a gift waiting for me in the imaginal space of the Twilight Threshold. I loosened my grip on a problem and was able to open to an improved relationship with my writing. It was up to me to notice the shift and follow through on my book. With renewed energy, I reconnected with my purpose to write. The magic of the liminal space is that our minds can creatively crack open a problem and find the surprises that our souls crave.

Conclusion

You have immense potential to activate change in your life when you unwrap the gifts of your dreams and the Twilight Threshold. Remember that the dreamers in this book crossed into an imaginal realm and gained insight into their lives in ways that they would not have otherwise. The stories in this book illustrate the value of dreams and how they can lead you through a portal to live your life with more joy, compassion, and fun. They also illuminate the magic that can occur in your waking life when you insert your personal authority into a dream or the imaginal realm.

To take your learning further, my website has additional resources to help you on your path with dreams. This includes an audio meditation that can help you reach the imaginal realm so that you can return to the physical world with juicy wisdom. I also offer a workbook with a dream journal. Charts are included, much like in this book, so that you can easily practice all you learn here. https://kb.kirstenbridge.com/book-downloads

The only person that will grant you the freedom to access the mystical realm is you. When you make a habit of using these intuitive practices, you harvest the messages waiting to support you on your journey. In turn, you create a way of leading your life that embraces both the mystical and rational qualities in you.

May these dreaming practices support you to create a more nourishing life.

Notes

Notes

Notes

Notes

Notes

www.ingramcontent.com/pod-product-compliance
Lightning Source LLC
Chambersburg PA
CBHW062054290426
44109CB00027B/2822